Contents

Say the sounds

w x y ch sh th ng ai ee
oa oo ar or ur ow oi er

What is pond dipping?

Pond dipping is a lot of fun.

You dip a net into a pond,
and catch animals in the water.

This book tells you how to do it.

What do you need?

net

an adult

lens

boots

You don't need much
to go pond dipping.

box

plastic spoon

pond book

pen and pad

A good pond

Now you need to look for a good pond.

Good pond

A flat bank.

No mud to slip on.

Get dipping!

Fill the box with water.

Dip the net into the pond.

Lift it out, and tip the contents into the box.

What did you catch?

Look at the animals in the box.

What is it?

Look for the animal
in a pond book.

The book will tell you what it is.
Can you see the water boatman?

Pond Animals

frog

water boatman

water snail

Back in the pond

Put all the animals
back in the water.

When you go pond dipping again, they are sure to be there!

Glossary

 bank

 bug box

 frog

 lens

 net

 water

 water boatman

 water snail